420.24
W458
Spanish

27 Phrasal Verbs Que Debes Conocer

Libro bilingüe para aprender y practicar los phrasal verbs más importantes del inglés.

Daniel Welsch

27 Phrasal Verbs Que Debes Conocer

Libro bilingüe para aprender y practicar los phrasal verbs más importantes del inglés.

by Daniel Welsch

Tercera Edición, Julio 2013

Copyright © Daniel Welsch 2013.

Aprende más inglés en http://madridingles.es

Diseño de cubierta por Lucy Moretti

http://lucymorettidesign.tumblr.com

CONTENIDO

Introducción	7
La Gramática de los Phrasal Verbs	11
Los 27 Phrasal Verbs	17
Conversaciones	59
Ejercicios	64
Respuestas	76
Acerca del Autor	79

INTRODUCCIÓN

POR QUÉ HAS ESCRITO ESTE LIBRO?

He escrito este libro porque enseño el inglés desde hace casi una década y me he dado cuenta que la manera estándar de enseñar los phrasal verbs no funciona.

En los libros de texto que utilizo, hay una introducción a los phrasal verbs para el nivel pre-intermedio. Se supone que la gente llega a estudiarlo con un año y medio de clase a sus espaldas.

Pero si hago la prueba dándo estos mismos phrasal verbs a mis alumnos del nivel avanzado (que llevan ya de 5 a 10 años estudiando), resulta que tampoco los saben, normalmente. La razón es que los libros de texto dan una lista de phrasal verbs tras otra, sin ningún contexto y sin ningún repaso, suponen que la gente ve una combinación una vez y ya la tiene memorizada sin más.

Si mis estudiantes en Madrid necesitan mucho más tiempo para practicar los phrasal verbs, seguro que otros estudiantes del inglés en otros países también.

Aquí quiero abarcar al tema de los phrasal verbs de otra manera, para asegurar que conoces unos muy bien antes de seguir con otros.

QUÉ ES UN PHRASAL VERB?

Un phrasal verb es un verbo que va seguido de una partícula. La partícula es una preposición o un adverbio que cambia el significado del verbo. Da dirección al verbo (adverbial phrase) o otro significado distinto al verbo original (phrasal verb).

Aquí no diferencio mucho, aunque algunos libros lo hacen, entre adverbial phrases y phrasal verbs. La cuestión es que la partícula da una información importante, cambiando el significado del verbo.

REALMENTE SE USAN LOS PHRASAL VERBS?

Sí. Se usan todos los días. Más en conversación que escrito.

Algunas ideas son muy difíciles (o incluso imposibles) de explicar sin phrasal verbs. Otras se pueden expresar usando otras palabras, pero la gente suele usar el phrasal verb.

Incluso si no usas muchos phrasal verbs al hablar, es imprescindible entenderlos. Son una parte importante del idioma que cualquier nativo usa sin pensar. Incluso muchos nativos piensan que es más fácil entenderles si usan palabras pequeñas. Así dicen *"Let's get on with it"* cuando sería mucho más fácil para un hispanohablante entender *"Let's continue."*

CUÁL ES LA MEJOR MANERA DE APRENDERLOS?

Muchos libros dan un ejemplo o dos de un phrasal verb y dan por hecho que lo has aprendido. La realidad es que una persona necesita alrededor de 7 ejemplos para memorizar algo. Las palabras cobran significado cuando las vemos en una variedad de contextos. Por eso, en este libro, doy relativamente pocos verbos, con muchos ejemplos y ejercicios.

Es mejor hacer pocas cosas y hacerlas bien que hacer muchas cosas y hacerlas mal!

Es imprescindible volver a estudiar las mismas cosas varias veces. La repetición no es lo más divertido del mundo, pero sirve para aprender cualquier cosa que uno se plantea en esta vida.

CUANTOS PHRASAL VERBS TENGO QUE CONOCER?

De hecho, hay más de 1000 phrasal verbs en el inglés, pero un estudiante no-nativo no tiene por qué saberse todos. Estaría bien saber unos 100. En eso es como los verbos irregulares: hay muchos que vas a ver una vez al año y sería mejor no aprenderlos. Usa tu tiempo para aprender los phrasal verbs que vas a escuchar todos los días, como los que están en este libro.

COMO USAR ESTE LIBRO

Como dije antes, la repetición es lo que te ayuda a memorizar algo. Estudia un par de phrasal verbs un día. Vuelve a repetirlos el día siguiente, y repásalos al cabo de una semana y al cabo del mes. Son cuatro repeticiones (de varios ejemplos de cada phrasal verb), lo cual te da bastante para que entre en la memoria a largo plazo. Al final del libro hay unos ejercicios que consisten en colocar la preposición correcta en la frase que también te ayudarán a recordarlos.

LA GRAMÁTICA DE LOS PHRASAL VERBS

Los phrasal verbs tienen unas reglas propias que tienes que saber para usarlos bien.

Primero, lo que siempre tenemos que tener en cuenta es que la partícula es igual que importante que el verbo.

Pongamos un ejemplo:

Él está mirando a Susan. = *He's looking at Susan.*

Él está buscando a Susan. = *He's looking for Susan.*

Entre *look at* y *look for* hay una enorme diferencia, en español incluso se dicen con verbos distintos.

Otro ejemplo:

Enciende la televisión. = *Turn on the TV*

Apaga la televisión. = *Turn off the TV.*

Aquí la diferencia entre encender y apagar es la preposición, *on* o *off*. Pero tenemos también:

Sube el volúmen a la televisión. = *Turn up the TV.*

Baja el volúmen a la televisión. = *Turn down the TV.*

O sea que tenemos, como minimo, cuatro phrasal verbs con *turn* que se pueden aplicar a una televisión!

Hay más que se debe saber sobre phrasal verbs.

TRANSITIVOS Y INTRANSITIVOS

Los hay transitivos y intransitivos. O sea, que unos aceptan un complemento y otros no. Por ejemplo:

Quítate la chaqueta. = *Take off your jacket.*

Aquí *take off* es transitivo (el complemento es *your jacket*)

El avión despega a las 3:30. = *The plane takes off at 3:30.*

Aquí *take off* es intransitivo. El avión despega, simplemente, y no acepta un complemento.

Este ejemplo, take off, puede ser intransitivo o transitivo, dependiendo del contexto, pero hay otros que son siempre uno o el otro.

I'm looking after my nephew tonight. = transitivo (el complemento es mi sobrino, y la frase no tendría sentido sin él).

SEPARABLES Y INSEPARABLES

Los hay separables, y los hay no separables. O sea, que algunos no se molestan si separas la partícula del verbo, poniendo el complemento en medio. (Claro que si el phrasal verb es intransitivo, no tiene complemento y no puede separarse para poner el complemento en medio.)

Separables:

I'm putting my jacket on.

He's taking his shoes off.

They're trying to work the problem out.

Inseparables:

I'm looking for an apartment.

She's looking after her sister.

He got rid of his old books.

Cuando usamos un pronombre (me, you, him, her, it, us, them) como complemento de un phrasal verb separable, tenemos que separarlo.

Por ejemplo:

I'm putting on my jacket. = I'm putting it on.

He's taking off his shoes. = He's taking them off.

They're trying to work out the problem. = They're trying to work it out.

Si usamos un pronombre con un phrasal verb inseparable, obviamente, no separamos.

Ejemplos:

She's looking after him.

He got rid of them.

I'm looking for it.

LOS PHRASAL VERBS Y LOS TIEMPOS VERBALES

Aparte de eso, los phrasal verbs siguen todas las otras reglas de los tiempos verbales, se hacen negaciones y preguntas con ellos y se les ponen verbos auxiliares.

El primer phrasal verb que veremos es el famoso get up, que significa levantarse, aquí daré unos sencillos ejemplos de cómo usarlo en varios tiempos verbales.

Pasado simple: I got up early this morning.

Futuro (going to): I'm going to get up early tomorrow.

Pasado simple (pregunta): What time did you get up yesterday?

Presente simple (tercera persona): She usually gets up at 8 o'clock.

Presente simple (pregunta): What time does she usually get up?

Presente perfecto: I have gotten up at 8 o'clock every day this week.

Y así sucesivamente con los demás tiempos verbales.

LOS 27 PHRASAL VERBS

Estos son 27 de los phrasal verbs más importantes del inglés. Algunos están organizados junto con otro parecido, o uno con significado opuesto.

GET UP / WAKE UP

get up = levantarse. **wake up** = despertarse. Hay una clara diferencia entre estos dos phrasal verbs. **Get up** es levantarse de la cama, mientras que **wake up** es simplemente despertarse. Uno puede despertarse, y luego quedarse en la cama durante horas. Dormirse se dice **go to sleep**.

She woke up at 9 o'clock, but stayed in bed all morning. When she finally got up, it was lunch time.

I always get up at 7 AM. I don't mind waking up early.

What time do you usually get up?

I went to sleep late last night, so I got up late this morning.

I woke up at six o'clock, but I didn't get up until almost seven. That's why I'm late.

I set my alarm to wake me up on time for work.

The shouting in the street was loud enough to wake me up, but I didn't get up to see what was happening.

You should wake Mary up. It's almost time for breakfast.

(In a hotel) I ordered a wake-up call for six thirty. That should give us time to get to the airport.

I hope I didn't wake you up when I arrived. Did I make a lot of noise?

Glosario:

loud enough = lo bastante alto (de volumen)

a wake up call = una llamada para despertar a alguien

I don't mind = no me importa, no me molesta

Escribe unos ejemplos originales:

_____

_____

_____

_____

_____

GO OUT

to go out = salir para ir a un evento social. **to go out with someone** = tener una relación (más o menos) romántica con alguien. **to stay in** = quedarse en casa, **come/go home** = volver a casa.

I don't really feel like going out. Why don't we stay in and make a pizza.

Is Susan going out with anyone at the moment?

She's just started going out with a guy she met on holiday.

They've been going out since high school.

I usually go out on Saturday nights. Friday nights I stay in.

He went out last night, and came home late, so today he's very tired.

Let's go out for a drink! Do you want to have a mojito?

Glosario:

high school = el instituto (educación secundaria)

feel like doing something = tener ganas de hacer algo, apetecer

Escribe unos ejemplos originales:

_____

_____

_____

_____

_____

LOOK AFTER

to look after someone/something = cuidar a algo o alguien, especialmente un niño

He's looking after my plants while I'm away on holiday.

Could you look after the baby tomorrow night while I'm out?

I don't mind looking after your dog, but I don't like looking after cats.

He always asks his sister to look after the kids on Saturdays.

While I was busy looking after Jimmy, Sally fell down and cut her knee.

If you get a babysitter to look after the kids, we can go out.

My aunt used to come over and look after my sister and I every morning.

Glosario:

babysitter = niñera

come over = ir a la casa de alguien

Escribe unos ejemplos originales:

GET ON

to get on with someone = llevarse bien con alguien. Inseparable y transitivo.

Si va en negativo, significa llevarse mal. También acepta adverbios (well, very well, pretty well, extremely well, better, best, etc) entre las partículas **on** y **with**.

She doesn't get on very well with her boss, but she gets on extremely well with her coworkers.

Do you get on with your parents?

How do you get on with your classmates?

I've been getting on better with my mother the last few years.

I get on pretty well with all my cousins, but I get on best with my cousin Phil.

I don't get on terribly well with people like him. He's so annoying!

Glosario:

annoying = molesto

classmates = compañeros de clase

coworkers = compañeros de trabajo. En inglés británico, se dicen **workmates.**

Escribe unos ejemplos originales:

_____

_____

_____

_____

_____

PUT ON / TAKE OFF

to put something on = ponerse una prenda, etc. **to take something off** = quitar una prenda, etc.

He took off his jacket and hung it up behind the door.

You should take off your hat in the Cathedral.

In many countries, it's customary to take off your shoes when you go in the house. In winter, people put on slippers to keep their feet warm.

Why don't you put on your raincoat? You're getting wet!

Did you put on sunblock when you went to the beach? You're sunburnt!

If I take off my glasses, I won't be able to read the newspaper.

She put on her gloves so she wouldn't get her hands dirty in the garden.

take off = despegar (un avión) Lo contrario es **land** o **touch down**.

Sorry for the delay, the plane will be taking off in just a few minutes.

In the end, the plane took off almost an hour late. We just landed a few minutes ago

Glosario:

delay = retraso

sunburnt = quemado por el sol

sunblock = crema solar

slippers = zapatillas para andar en casa

hang something up = colgar algo

keep something warm = mantener algo caliente

Escribe unos ejemplos originales:

_____

_____

_____

_____

_____

TURN ON / TURN OFF

turn on = encender un aparato eléctrico **turn off** = apagar un aparato eléctrico. Muchas veces un ordenador dice **shut down** en vez de **turn off**.

You should turn off your mobile if you're going to sleep. You don't want it to wake you up.

She opened the door and turned on the light.

The lights are programmed to turn off automatically after a minute.

We should turn on the air conditioning. It's getting hot.

I'm going to turn off the stove. The soup is cooked.

If you turn off the heating when you leave, you'll save electricity.

Could you turn off the TV? I'm finished watching it.

Have you already turned on the computer?

Glosario

air conditioning = aire acondicionado

save electricity = ahorrar en electricidad

soup = sopa

cooked = cocinado

programmed = programado

Escribe unos ejemplos originales:

_____

_____

_____

_____

_____

START OUT / END UP

start out = empezar un proceso, un viaje, etc. **end up** = acabar, terminar un proceso, llegar a un punto.

He started out studying to be a lawyer, but he ended up working as a teacher.

We started out at home, and after an hour walking, we ended up in the town center.

When he started out writing songs, he never imagined he'd end up being in a band.

I started out thinking I was going to go to New York, but I ended up going to Istanbul.

Eventually he ended up living with his mother again, at age 50.

The day started out well, but I had a bad headache in the afternoon.

When I started out, I imagined it would be a lot easier.

I wanted to go out, but finally I ended up staying home.

Glosario:

lawyer = abogado

headache = dolor de cabeza

stay home = quedarse en casa

Escribe unos ejemplos originales:

_____

_____

_____

_____

TURN UP / TURN DOWN

turn up = subir (el volumen, la calefacción, etc) **turn down** = bajar (el volumen, la calefacción, etc.) Ambos phrasal verbs se utilizan principalmente con aparatos electrónicos.

Could you please turn down the music? I can't sleep!

If we turn up the heat, we'll be more comfortable. It must be below freezing outside.

She turned down the volume on her mp3 player so she could concentrate better.

He turned up the TV when his favorite music video came on.

turn up tiene otro significado: aparecer (inesperadamente)

I was looking for the cat all afternoon, eventually she turned up under the sofa.

Her keys finally turned up, but by that time they'd already called a locksmith.

turn down también tiene otro significado: rechazar.

He asked her out several times, but she always turned him down.

He found out that his visa application had been turned down yesterday.

Glosario:

freezing = helado (viene del verbo **freeze**, que quiere decir congelar)

eventually = al final (fíjate que **NO** significa eventualmente)

locksmith = cerrajero

visa = visado

Escribe unos ejemplos originales:

_____

_____

_____

_____

SET OUT / GET BACK

set out = partir, ir de viaje; **get back** = volver de viaje, o simplemente volver. El sentido normal de irse o salir se expresa con **go** o **leave**.

If we set out early, we'll get back before dinner.

What time did you get back from your trip?

He left for work early in the morning, and didn't get back until 11 o'clock at night.

The bus gets back to town around 6. Can you come to the station to pick me up?

We should set out before lunch, that way we'll miss the traffic.

The earlier we set out, the earlier we'll arrive.

He's gone out for a moment. I'll talk to him as soon as he gets back.

Could you tell her to call me when she gets back?

Glosario:

trip = viaje. Recuérdate que travel siempre es el verbo!

pick someone up = recoger a alguien.

Escribe unos ejemplos originales:

_____

_____

_____

_____

_____

BREAK UP

break up with someone = terminar una relación romántica, separarse, romper. Es transitivo y inseparable, añadiendo la persona despues de una segunda preposición **with**. Si se usa **we broke up** o **they broke up** no se usa el **with someone**.

Have you heard? Susan broke up with her boyfriend this weekend.

Tom has been a bit depressed since Kate broke up with him.

Bill is thinking about breaking up with his girlfriend.

Don't worry if he breaks up with you. You'll find someone new.

Sam is so strange! He's always falling in love with girls, then breaking up with them a coupe of weeks later.

I was sad when we broke up, but now I think it's for the best.

When she met him, she hadn't yet broken up with her previous boyfriend.

Glosario:

depressed = deprimido

fall in love = enamorarse. El verbo **fall**, literalmente, es caer, lo cual hace que **fall in love** parezca un accidente. Pero bueno.

Escribe unos ejemplos originales:

_____

_____

_____

_____

BREAK DOWN

break down = romperse, averiarse (un vehículo, una máquina grande). Es intransitivo y inseparable.

When the train broke down, we had to wait for 3 hours to continue on our journey.

His car broke down when he was on holiday, and he had to take it to the mechanic.

Did it break down on when he was leaving, or on the way back?

If your car breaks down, you'll have to call the tow truck.

When one of the factory's machines broke down, they had to stop working and fix it.

My old Chevrolet has broken down so many times I don't trust it anymore.

He had to spend the afternoon fixing his motorcycle after it broke down.

Glosario:

journey = viaje (especialment un viaje largo)

tow truck = grua. El verbo tow es remolcar.

trust = fiarse, confiar en algo

Escribe unos ejemplos originales:

_____

_____

_____

_____

_____

GET RID OF

get rid of something = deshacerte de algo. Es transitivo y inseparable. La palabra **rid** es parte necesaria de la expresión, sólo se usa en este phrasal verb en el inglés moderno.

When she got rid of her car, she started taking public transport a lot more.

I have some old clothes I want to get rid of. Do you know who I can donate them to?

I really want to get rid of all these books. They're cluttering up my room.

Do you think we should get rid of these tools? We hardly ever use them.

I've already lost a lot of weight, but I can't seem to get rid of these last few kilos.

I got rid of a lot of stuff by selling it online.

I think you'd be better off if you got rid of your old car and bought a newer one.

Glosario:

to be better off = estar mejor

clutter = desorden

stuff = cosas (incontable). Si queremos decir algo contable, usamos **things.**

Escribe unos ejemplos originales:

_____

_____

_____

_____

_____

WORK OUT

work something out = solucionar un problema, calcular. Así usado es transitivo, y separable. Acúerdate de la canción de the Beatles que se llama *We Can Work It Out*, que habla de la posibilidad de solucionar los problemas que tiene una pareja.

They've been trying to work out the problems with their computer all day.

Hopefully he and his girlfriend can work everything out. They've been having a difficult time lately.

Did you work out how much we have to pay in taxes?

In the end everything worked out fine, and we could forget about the whole thing.

work out = hacer deporte. Así usado es intransitivo.

He always works out three times a week. That's why he's so thin.

After I work out at the gym, I always like to eat a big lunch.

Working out makes me feel great! Whenever I'm feeling a little bit down I go for a run.

Professional athletes spend several hours each day working out.

Glosario:

athletes = deportistas (en general, no sólo los que hacen atletismo)

taxes = impuestos

to feel down = sentirse mal

Escribe unos ejemplos originales:

_____

_____

_____

_____

MAKE UP

make something up = inventar una historia, una mentira, una excusa, etc. Así es separable y transitivo.

That story was a lie. She made the whole thing up.

Is that the best excuse you can make up? They'll never believe us!

She made that whole story up. None of it is true.

make up a class, an exam, etc = recuperar

I didn't take the test last week, so I'm making it up this week.

If class is cancelled, we'll make up the lost time another day.

If you fail this exam, you have to make it up next semester.

make up your mind = decidir

He's having trouble making up his mind about what to study at university.

I've made up my mind: I'm moving to Germany.

make someone/yourself up = maquillarse. Normalmente, en todo caso, se dice **put on make-up.** Así usado es transitivo y separable. Con guión, **make-up** es el sustantivo: maquillaje.

She's in the bathroom, making herself up.

She put on some make-up before going out.

Do you always put on make-up before work?

Glosario:

trouble = problemas, dificultades (incontable)

lie = mentir

Escribe unos ejemplos originales:

_____

_____

_____

_____

GIVE UP

give something up = dejar de hacer algo que hacemos habitualmente, especialmente algo que nos gusta. Así es transitivo y separable

She smoked for over 20 years, but finally she gave it up a few months ago.

He's given up sweets because his doctor told him he has to lose weight.

I'm giving up my job to go back to university.

give up = rendirse, abandonar el esfuerzo, entregarse a la policia

I tried to learn Chinese for a few months, but eventually I gave up. It was too difficult.

When they realized they were trapped, the robbers gave themselves up.

I give up! It's impossible to argue with you.

He's very stubborn. Once he starts something, he never gives up.

Glosario:

stubborn = cabezota

argue = discutir

robbers = ladrones

sweets = dulces

trapped = atrapado

Escribe unos ejemplos originales:

_____

_____

_____

_____

_____

GROW UP

grow up = hacerse adulto, y en un sentido más amplio, pasar la niñez. Es intransitivo. Para decir crecer, usamos, simplemente, **grow**. Para hablar de plantas y animales usamos siempre **grow**, sin la partícula: *The corn is growing in the fields.*

I grew up in Chicago, and I moved to Washington to go to college.

They wanted their kids to grow up in a safe neighborhood, so they moved out of the city.

He was born in France, but grew up in Germany. His parents, on the other hand, grew up in the United States.

After growing up in a strict religious environment, he stopped going to church.

Look at how our daughter is growing up! She's already interested in boys.

She's an old friend from the neighborhood where I grew up.

Glosario:

neighborhood = barrio

church = iglesia

college = en inglés americano, se usa **college** para decir universidad.

Escribe unos ejemplos originales:

_____

_____

_____

_____

_____

LOOK FORWARD TO

look forward to something = esperar algo con ilusión, tener muchas ganas de algo que pasará en el futuro. En las series de televisión americanas, **"I'm looking forward to..."** se traduce muchas veces como "No veo el momento de..." Se usa mucho en presente continuo, seguido de un sustantivo o un gerundio, lo cual lo hace transitivo.

I'm really looking forward to seeing you tomorrow.

She's looking forward to the wedding. It's her big day.

Are you looking forward to going on holiday next week?

My father's looking forward to his retirement. He's 65 next year.

What he's really looking forward to is having more time to read.

I'm going to Australia next month. I'm really looking forward to it.

I'm looking forward to finishing university so I can start working.

What are you looking forward to doing this weekend?

I'm looking forward to seeing my friends.

Glosario:

retirement = jubilación

wedding = boda

Escribe unos ejemplos originales:

_____

_____

_____

_____

PUT UP WITH

put up with something/someone = soportar a algo/alguien. En negativo solemos usar **can't stand someone/something**. *I can't stand you!* = No te soporto!

After putting up with the noise for an hour, I called the police.

I guess we'll just have to put up with the mosquitos. I can't stand her! How do you manage to put up with her so well?

I don't know how long I'll be able to put up with all these house guests.

I don't understand how she puts up with her son. He's such a pain!

I'm getting used to the cold weather. I guess I'm learning how to put up with it.

Are you going to put up with her forever? Or are you going to ask her to stop behaving that way?

Glosario:

get used to something = acostumbrarse a algo

behave = comportarse

to be a pain = ser molesto

manage = apañarse

noise = ruido

Escribe unos ejemplos originales:

_____

_____

_____

_____

TRY ON

try something on = probarse una prenda de vestir. Se usa **try** sin partícula para hablar de actividades, comida etc... todo lo que no es ropa.

I'd like to try on this shirt, please. In medium, if you have one.

You should try on that jacket. I bet it looks great on you.

She tried on a few wedding dresses, but didn't find anything she liked.

I tried it on and it was a little too big. Do you have a smaller size?

Why don't you try on a bigger pair? Those look uncomfortable.

I feel like I've already tried on everything in the store!

Glosario:

pair = par (de zapatos, etc)

jacket = chaqueta

shirt = camisa

uncomfortable = incómodo

wedding dress = vestido de novia

Escribe unos ejemplos originales:

_____

_____

_____

_____

_____

PUT IN / TAKE OUT

put something in = poner algo dentro, introducir algo.

take something out = sacar algo. Las dos preposiciones **in / out** son opuestas y en este caso indican direcciones contrarias.

When you put the beer in the fridge, take out a bottle of water.

I'm going to put these clothes in the closet.

I'm going to take some money out of the bank.

Can you put my keys in your bag?

She put a few liters of petrol in the car yesterday.

If you take a few things out of the trunk, you'll have more space for your luggage.

She took the towels out of the cupboard and put them in the bathroom.

Glosario:

closet = armario (empotrado, normalmente)

trunk = maletero del coche

cupboard = armario (no empotrado)

luggage = equipaje

fridge = frigorífico

Escribe unos ejemplos originales:

_____

_____

_____

_____

_____

CONVERSACIONES

Estas conversaciones utilizan los 27 phrasal verbs que hemos visto hasta ahora.

John and Susan

John: What time did you get up this morning, Susan?
Susan: I got up at eleven o'clock.
John: Eleven o'clock! Why? Did you go out last night?
Susan: Yes, I went out and I didn't get back home until early this morning.
John: I worked out at the gym yesterday, so I went to bed early.
Susan: Do you want to go out tonight?
John: No, I can't. I have to stay home and look after my niece.
Susan: Oh of course! She's so cute... She must really be growing up.
John: She'll be 10 next month.
Susan: Does she get on well with her brother?
John: More or less. They're kids, so they have their arguments!
Susan: Well, maybe we can go out another night.
John: Next weekend would be great... If I don't end up looking after my niece again.

Anna and Pablo

Pablo: Hey Anna! Have you heard the news?
Anna: What news?
Pablo: Melissa broke up with her boyfriend!
Anna: Oh, really?
Pablo: Yes! Finally...
Anna: You used to go out with Melissa, didn't you?
Pablo: Yes, I did.
Anna: But then she started going out with Tony.
Pablo: Unfortunately.
Anna: They were going out for a long time, weren't they?
Pablo: Yes. I don't know how she put up with him for so long.
Anna: And now that she's broken up with Tony, you think she might go out with you again...
Pablo: It's possible!
Anna: Well, good luck!
Pablo: I've always got on very well with her.
Anna: Yes, well, maybe you'll end up getting married and having lots of children together.
Pablo: Yes, maybe we will!
Anna: I'm looking forward to going to your wedding, then.
Pablo: Ah yes. Me, too!

Richard and Laura

Richard: I'm really looking forward to our holiday. What time should we set out tomorrow?

Laura: I guess if we leave at 7 o'clock, we'll end up at the airport around 8.

Richard: So we have to wake up around 5:30.

Laura: I'm going to set my alarm to wake me up at 5:15. Just in case.

Richard: What time does the plane take off?

Laura: At 9:30.

Richard: Great. Did you put the tickets in your purse?

Laura: Yeah, I have them.

Richard: And did you put everything else in your suitcase?

Laura: Yes, I packed my suitcase.

Richard: And your sister is coming to look after the cat while we're away?

Laura: Yes, she's going to come every day. until we get back.

Richard: You know, when we get back, we have to wait 6 months for our next holiday.

Laura: Yes, I'm not looking forward to going back to work.

Tony and Kate

Tony: Hey Kate. Did I tell you that I've given up smoking?
Kate: Oh, congratulations.
Tony: I've given up before, of course.
Kate: Really?
Tony: Yeah. Last time I ended up smoking again after about 6 months.
Kate: Quitting is hard.
Tony: Yeah. But this time I'm really going to do it. I'm also going to start working out.
Kate: Working out? But you hate exercising!
Tony: I know. But I need to start. After Melissa broke up with me, I realized I have to change.
Kate: Oh yeah, Melissa. She's not very nice. I don't know how you put up with her!
Tony: Well, she's very beautiful.
Kate: If you say so. Anyway, what's she doing these days?
Tony: She ended up going out with her ex-boyfriend Pablo again.
Kate: Pablo?
Tony: Yeah. Pablo works out all the time. He's got really big muscles. And he gave up smoking years ago.
Kate: Good for Pablo.

Bob and Bill

Bob: Hey Bill.

Bill: Hi Bob. How's it going?

Bob: I'm angry!

Bill: Why?

Bob: My car broke down last night!

Bill: Oh no!

Bob: I just got back from the mechanic's, and he says it's going to cost me a thousand dollars to fix it.

Bill: That's a lot of money. Why did it break down?

Bob: Apparently there was a leak somewhere. All the oil dripped out.

Bill: That's no good.

Bob: No, it isn't. I just put some oil in a couple of weeks ago. So now I've damaged the engine.

Bill: Uh oh.

Bob: I guess I'll end up buying a new car soon.

Bill: Do you have the money for that?

Bob: More or less. I'll have to take some money out of my savings account. And I might have to give up going on vacation this year. But it'll be okay.

EXERCISES 1

Une las dos partes de las frases.

1. I'd like to try
2. He's looking
3. I had to get
4. The noise woke
5. I'm going to put the food
6. She doesn't get

on very well with her boss.
in the fridge.
on this sweater, please.
up at 5 AM today.
after my cat while I'm away.
him up.

7. She grew
8. They took
9. I turned
10. We got
11. He broke
12. They set

out very early in the morning.
off the TV and went to bed.
off their shoes.
up with his girlfriend.
back very late.
up in a small town.

13. The plane took
14. He ended
15. She put
16. I'm looking forward
17. I just turned
18. The car broke

to going on holiday.
on her coat.
off an hour ago.
on the radio.
down outside the city.
up working as a waiter.

19. Could you turn up with Tony?
20. Do you want to go up in the USA?
21. What time will we get back tomorrow?
22. How do you put up down the music?
23. Did you grow with the rain every day?
24. Why did Melissa break out tonight?

25. I didn't turn the story up.
26. It's true. I didn't make on the lights.
27. I don't want to get rid off my hat.
28. I'm not going to take after the children.
29. She isn't looking out. I don't have any money.
30. I can't go of these books.

31. He started out working in a bank.
32. I can't work on very well.
33. Did you put the money in the bank?
34. They don't get out a solution to the problem.
35. Could you take the fish forward to Christmas.
36. The children are looking out of the freezer?

EXERCISES 2

Pon la partícula correcta. En el caso de phrasal verbs con dos partículas, solo falta una.

1. He's really looking _____ to going to Vietnam this year.

2. They were born in Sweden, but they grew _____ in Denmark.

3. I have to get _____ early tomorrow to go to the airport. I'll probably wake _____ around 6.

4. She's been going _____ with her boyfriend for several years, I think they'll get married soon.

5. Why don't you put _____ a tie? You'll look more formal.

6. She turned _____ the light and soon fell asleep.

7. He gets _____ very well with his mother, it's his father who's the problem.

8. Could you look _____ my cats while I'm away?

9. I think that sweater would look great on you. Why don't you try it _____?

10. Take your passport _____ of your bag, you need to show it to the Customs officer.

11. I've tried putting _____ with her and I can't. She's just too annoying!

12. I think I'm going to give _____ my aerobics class for now. I just don't have time.

13. I don't believe anything she said. I think she's making the whole thing _____.

14. We're going to set _____ at around 9 o'clock. That way we'll arrive before lunch.

15. If we leave early, we'll get _____ before dark.

16. Sarah and Jimmy broke _____ when he moved to a new city.

17. They offered him a job in Germany, but he turned it _____.

18. I have a storeroom full of stuff I want to get rid _____. Do you know any charity that will come pick it up?

19. I'm going to the gym later. I want to work _____ before dinner.

20. She started _____ working as a secretary, but ended _____ as manager.

21. Don't worry about looking for those papers. I'm sure they'll turn _____ somewhere.

22. Could you turn _____ the volume on the TV? I'm trying to sleep!

23. Their whole family gets _____ so well. It seems like they never fight.

24. Her car broke _____ when she was driving cross country, so she had to take a plane.

25. I'm going to turn _____ the TV. I want to see the news.

26. Take _____ your sunglasses. You look like an idiot wearing them indoors.

27. You should put the eggs _____ the fridge. You don't want to leave them out too long.

28. My grandfather gave _____ drinking when he was in his fifties, and he never touched a bottle again.

29. If you get _____ a little earlier, you'll definitely make it to work on time.

30. Can you turn _____ the heating? It's getting really hot in here.

31. The band started _____ playing jazz, but switched to blues after a few months.

32. Could we get rid _____ some of these empty bottles? We're not using them for anything.

33. She's all made _____ because she's going dancing later.

34. His parents always spoke French while he was growing _____. That's why he's bilingual.

35. I'm really looking _____ to seeing you this weekend.

36. We wanted to go _____, but it was raining so hard that we ended _____ staying in.

37. They got a babysitter to look _____ their children while they're away.

38. I love this song! Turn it _____!

39. She has to get _____ early because she starts work at eight.

40. You should put the white wine _____ the fridge so it'll be cold by the time we eat. And while you're in the fridge, take _____ a bottle of water, will you?

41. His first book was rejected by several publishers, but it ended _____ selling a lot of copies.

42. I turned _____ the job offer because the salary was worse than at my current job.

43. I was looking for my other shoe for what seemed like an hour. Finally it turned _____ under the sofa.

44. They've been going _____ for a few weeks. They met at Will's party.

45. She broke _____ with her boyfriend after a big argument they had on their anniversary.

46. I grew _____ in a small town, but now I love the big city.

47. If you give _____ smoking, you'll feel a lot better.

48. I set my alarm to wake me _____ at 7:30.

49. I tried _____ three or four pairs of shoes, but none of them were very comfortable.

50. My Canadian friends always take _____ their shoes when they're at home.

51. I'm going to put _____ my boots. There's a lot of snow on the ground.

52. He's been working _____ a lot because he wants to lose weight.

53. If you turn _____ the router and wait a minute before turning it back _____, you can reset it.

54. Put _____ a scarf or you'll catch cold.

55. I get _____ with most of my neighbors, but there is one who's just a pain in the neck.

56. You should turn _____ the lights to save electricity.

57. If you put _____ some moisturizer after you're out in the sun, your skin will feel better.

58. Those trousers look a little small. You should try them _____ before you buy them.

59. I know that the professor is boring, but you'll just have to put _____ with him this semester.

60. The shouting in the street woke me _____ around four in the morning.

61. If my car breaks _____ I can call the tow truck. My insurance covers it.

62. I can't make _____ my mind--should I study engineering or architecture?

63. If you turn the oven _____ now, it'll have time to preheat while you're preparing the pizza.

64. He gave _____ his job last year to start his own business.

65. I tried to do that algebra problem, but I couldn't work _____ the answer.

66. After three years, they broke _____ last week. I guess they weren't happy together.

67. Are you looking forward _____ finishing your exams this semester?

68. She's setting _____ on her trip to South America tomorrow and she isn't getting _____ until next summer.

69. If you don't try to get _____ with your workmates, you'll have problems sooner or later.

70. He always looks _____ his health. He works _____ at the gym, eats healthy food, and goes running a couple times a week.

71. The plane takes _____ at half past four in the afternoon.

72. If you live here for a few years, you'll learn to put _____ with the heat.

73. The walk is about 20 kilometers, so if we set _____ at 10 o'clock, we'll be done by 3:00 or 4:00.

74. I like to turn _____ the radio when I'm home alone. It helps to have a little background noise.

75. You need to start acting like an adult! Grow _____!

76. The class that was cancelled last week will be made _____ this Friday.

77. He'll probably get _____ from work around six. He usually finishes at five.

78. I just put that money _____ the bank last week. I don't want to take it _____ now.

79. Your refrigerator is full of food you're never going to eat. Whey don't you get rid _____ it?

80. If you work _____ a couple days a week, you'll build some muscle.

81. I convinced her not to break _____ with her boyfriend for something so silly.

82. The meal started _____ with a bowl of gazpacho.

83. Columbus set _____ on his first voyage to America in 1492. He got _____ to Europe in 1493.

84. He's given _____ eating sweets because his doctor told him he has to lose weight.

85. The van broke _____ in the middle of the street, and a tow truck had to come to take it away.

86. He doesn't really get _____ with his mother-in-law, but they put _____ with each other.

87. I'm going to put _____ my raincoat. It looks pretty wet outside.

88. They're trying to get rid _____ some baby clothes now that their kids are a bit bigger.

89. I tried _____ a few different sizes until I found one that fit.

90. If you keep making noise, you'll wake the children _____.

91. The phone company turned _____ her internet connection because she didn't pay the bill.

Respuestas

Ejercicios 1

1. I'd like to try on this sweater, please.
2. He's looking after my cat while I'm away.
3. I had to get up at 5 AM today.
4. The noise woke him up.
5. I'm going to put the food in the fridge.
6. She doesn't get on very well with her boss.
7. She grew up in a small town.
8. They took off their shoes.
9. I turned off the TV and went to bed.
10. We got back very late.
11. He broke up with his girlfriend.
12. They set out very early in the morning.
13. The plane took off an hour ago.
14. He ended up working as a waiter.
15. She put on her coat.
16. I'm looking forward to going on holiday.
17. I just turned on the radio.
18. The car broke down outside the city.
19. Could you turn down the music?
20. Do you want to go out tonight?
21. What time will we get back tomorrow?
22. How do you put up with the rain every day?

23. Did you grow up in the USA?
24. Why did Melissa break up with Tony?
25. I didn't turn on the lights.
26. It's true. I didn't make the story up.
27. I don't want to get rid of these books.
28. I'm not going to take off my hat.
29. She isn't looking after the children
30. I can't go out. I don't have any money.
31. He started out working in a bank.
32. I can't work out a solution to the problem.
33. Did you put the money in the bank?
34. They don't get on very well.
35. Could you take the fish out of the freezer?
36. The children are looking forward to Christmas.

Ejercicios 2.

1. forward ... 2. up ... 3. up, up ... 4. out ... 5. on

6. off ... 7. on ... 8. after ... 9. on ... 10. out

11. up ... 12. up ... 13. up ... 14. out ... 15. back

16. up ...17. down ... 18. of ... 19. out ... 20. out, up

21. up ... 22. down ... 23. on ... 24. down ... 25. on

26. off ... 27. in ... 28. up ... 29. up ... 30. on

31. out ... 32. of ... 33. up ... 34. up ... 35. forward

36. out, up ... 37. after ... 38. up ... 39. up ... 40. in, out

41. up ... 42. down ... 43. up ... 44. out ... 45. up

46. up ... 47. up ... 48. up ... 49. on ... 50. off

51. on ... 52. out ... 53. off, on ... 54. on ... 55. on

56. off ... 57. on ... 58. on ... 59. up ... 60. up

61. down ... 62. up ... 63. on ... 64. up ... 65. out

66. up ... 67. to ... 68. out ... 69. on ... 70. after, out

71. off ... 72. up ... 73. out ... 74. on ... 75. up

76. up ... 77. back ... 78. in, out ... 79. of ... 80. out

81. up ... 82. out ... 83. out, back ... 84. up ... 85. down

86. on, up ... 87. on ... 88. of ... 89. on ... 90. up

91. off

ACERCA DEL AUTOR

Soy Daniel Welsch y llevo casi una década enseñando el inglés en Madrid. Escribo la página web http://madridingles.es donde puedes encontrar más de 600 artículos más sobre la gramática, el vocabulario, la pronunciación, los phrasal verbs y todo lo que tiene que ver con el inglés.

Mis otros libros incluyen ya han ayudado a miles de hispanohablantes a aprender más inglés: Incluyen *6 Claves Para Aprender Inglés*, *31 Phrasal Verbs Para Inglés de Negocios*, *Inglés Básico* y *Inglés Básico 2*.

6 Claves Para Aprender Inglés cuesta muy poco pero te ahorra mucho tiempo y esfuerzo a lo largo. Es una guía de estudio que habla de las 6 habilidades claves para ser bilingüe, y de como aprenderlas de la manera más rápida posible.

Ya ha ayudado a miles de hispanohablantes a enfocar sus estudios. Aquí tenéis lo que están diciendo algunos de los lectores:

Este libro te entrega las claves necesarias para poder entender la verdadera manera de como se aprende un idioma, Daniel Weisch expone con toda su experiencia en la vida las mejores pautas para ayudar a las personas a solucionar un problema de comunicación y entendimiento del idioma Inglés, Gracias Daniel.
Saludos.

—Robert

Excellent book for learning English, especially for Latinoamerican people. It has many interesting topics and realistic ways to practice the English language.

--Oscar

En realidad estas si son claves para aprender inglés, conforman un procedimiento práctico en lo cual uno debe centrarse y concentrarse para el aprendizaje de un idioma; es cierto que la Escuela y los Libros de Texto son una ayuda sobretodo para quien es principiante, pero las claves son sencillas, claras y objetivas se requiere ponerlas en práctica, lo cual demanda disciplina y constancia.

—Alonso

Made in the USA
Lexington, KY
27 August 2015